To my wife, Susan, my best friend and the love of my life, she made me who I am today.

and

.......To my pal, Vince Zandri, for his help and encouragement.

Cover Art: *Nairobi* by Susan Strazzella

Prologue

It is with trepidation that I begin this story. To write, it is something that I have always wanted to do, and now, I needed to do.

This story is not an autobiography, nor is it an historical fiction. It's a story about an ordinary life, nothing exciting,

It is a story about good and evil, fear, hope, family, friends, fate, God, faith and most assuredly, about love.

It's maybe a commentary about the world and what has happened to it; it is not the world I grew up in.

It is not a commentary on terrorism, or politics, although those topics will probably be noticed as a transparent undertone.

It is also about choices; and the life that revolves, and evolves around those choices.

It is about a mere 90 minutes of a life; a minuscule, indistinguishable fraction, really, out over 32 million minutes, (so Far).

But most of all, it is about what you learn from experiencing an horrific event, about yourself, about brave souls, about friends, about those you love, and what matters.

Humor me; laugh with me, cry with me, learn with me.

Chapter 1

…and now it begins

12:38PM – Nairobi, Kenya

….and now it begins, and I thought, maybe ends. Explosion.
Screaming. Panic. A grenade, unquestionably something the
average person doesn't hear every day. I had a fleeting
thought; wow, that was really loud. I look for Susan. She
followed directions and is crawling under a car bumper, also
something you don't see every day. I thought this is it; we are
going to die, not the way I thought. A really frightening
thought, a little surreal. Not panicked, but accepting. You have
an image of yourself alone, old and maybe sick, not being
shot in a mall parking garage in Nairobi, Kenya. I felt
surprisingly calm. However, deep humankind genetics jolt me
alert; flight or fright, time slows down, vision narrows,
decisions happen in micro seconds.

*"Life is an adventure, perilous indeed. But men are not meant
for safe havens. The fullness of life is in the hazards of life.
And, at the worst, there is that in us which can turn defeat into
victory."*   *Aeschylus*

Aeschylus, a Greek playwright, was the author of
"Prometheus Bound." I came across this quote a few years
ago. I felt at the time it exemplifies how I felt about life.

Moderation be damned, full steam ahead. But I digress again…

Did it ever happen to you, you are with some friends, after a long night of something, someone; "If you could do it over again, what would you change?" Wow, what a loaded question. Instantly everyone thinks of opportunities missed; women you should have slept with, women you shouldn't have, brainless mistakes, drunken escapades. But seriously, what would you change? Life is full of choices; some purposely made, some made for us. Life is seconds, inches; maybe millimeters.

12:15 PM…..…**13 minutes earlier**

The hotel driver pulls up in front of a modern, bustling mall. Earlier we had asked the hotel desk where we could spend the afternoon, kill some time, have a drink or two, a little shopping, experience the life of Nairobi. They suggested The Westgate Mall in downtown Nairobi, a short 15 minute drive. The five-story mall opened in 2007 and included 350,000 square feet of retail space and houses more than 80 stores, Nakumatt, a large grocery store, and Planet Media Cinemas anchor the mall. Other large stores include; Identity, Mr. Price, Home, Artcaffe, and Barclays Bank on the ground floor, and Millionaires Casino on the second floor. Smaller stores include outlets for international brands Adidas, Bata Shoes, Converse, FedEx, and Samsung Mobile.

The luxury shopping center is popular with Kenya's new consumer class, as well as foreign officials and expats. It was a beautiful Saturday afternoon, sunny and warm. There was also a kids cooking class event on the top floor garage, sponsored by a local radio station. It was going to be a fun afternoon.

We arrived to a busy entrance, mall cops, a bag scan, (a bag scan, odd but somewhat comforting) people in the crowded outdoor café by the door, a bustling and common scene. The driver gives us his cell number and we are out the door. The mall was at once familiar, a mall like all others.

It was a normal day; families, children. People were doing the normal Saturday afternoon things you might see in any mall in America, low background elevator music, laughter.

I was a child of the baby boomer generation, Born in Wilmington, Delaware to an Italian father, Adolph Francesco, and an Irish mother, Elizabeth Mary. I often remarked I got the best and worst of both, the wonderful loving sweetness, and hard headed obstinacy from Mom, and an extraordinary instant temper, hard work ethos and humor from Dad, an ordinary life. My childhood was like everyone else's, school, church, baseball; quite ordinary. It wasn't until I got older that I realized, hey, maybe not so ordinary in everything.

We learned my dad was a "stick it in your face" kinda guy; which I by the way loved and also turned out to be.

Chapter 2

Our Afternoon begins

12:20 PM

We enter the mall, and begin our stroll, what to do first; we first thought to have a coffee in the lobby coffee lounge. No, let's walk and have a beer or glass of wine later. Little did we realize, the monumental decision we just made.

12:25PM

On the first floor, essentially one floor below the entrance was Nakumatt, a large grocery store chain. I know it sounds weird, but I have visited grocery stores around the world. I was in that business for 32 years,

Starting out delivering Arnold bread on a truck in Baltimore, Maryland. I worked my way from those first days of 28 years old, to NYC, to Philadelphia, and left as VP Marketing. My boss of the last 17 years always wanted to visit stores. We looked at stores everywhere, from dawn to dusk, and sometimes later. It became habit, Susan put up with it, I loved it, even after retiring. It was an ordinary career; I worked hard, did the best I could.

12:27PM

We take a few steps inside the store, a normal, ordinary grocery store. The lights flicker. They flicker again and stay out. The cashiers are still working, no panic, must happen all the time. We decide to leave and come back; another crucial decision.

Mom was different, a red headed, blue eyed, Irish girl in the company of all the crazy Italians; plus, she could not cook. Unheard of, blasphemy! Despite the efforts of all the aunts, and Grandmom Strazzella, she just didn't get it. I came to realize, she just didn't care! Dad loved whatever she cooked. We thought that burnt, boiled to death, food was, well, normal. Mom was smart and funny, but overwhelmed by Dolphy, who was gregarious, loud and crazy.

A snapshot of an ordinary life; some craziness, but normal and ordinary. We didn't have a lot of money, dad worked 7 days a week, but we had what we needed, we didn't starve, we had food, a loving home, entertainment, but, the environment and loving nurture, created…a person who longed for adventure, excitement; me.

Chapter 3

Later that day and The later years

12:29PM

We ride the escalators on up the floors; relaxed and calm, taking it all in. Susan goes in a few stores, tries on tops, taking much longer than necessary. In the stores, clerks are bored; people are walking, unaware of what will happen in just a few minutes.

I was fortunate; I found a job at the university, working in the summer assigning dorm rooms. The director of "Dorm Assignments" was a retired US Marine, it was a crazy job; a 19 year old with long hair, working with a high and dry 50 year old Marine, somehow, he liked me? Little did I realize at the time, this job would be the lynch pin, the keystone, the very geneses of what my life will be.

Chapter 4

….and it begins, redux.

12:30PM

We are in the top floor Adidas store. Why? Well, the shoes Susan brought with her did not feel right…..so she bought a pair of Adidas in the airport in Addis Ababa, Ethiopia. Yes, in the airport in Addis Ababa, for some outrageous amount of money, and we were curious as to what the real price should be. (Also what the real Adidas should look like). I was on one side of the store, Susan another. Suddenly, we hear the unmistakable sound of gunfire. Unmistakable to me, I know gunfire, but the clerks in the store; clueless. This really can't be happening!!

After graduation, I was again blessed to get a job at the University "Housing & Residence Life" department. I had a free apartment on campus, a new car, money, but I never really left the safety of the university. I grew up fast here; but…something was missing, adventure, maybe? I had a stable job, but routine. This period in my life also become the creation of my life of choices. From here, I can chronicle the choices, those minuscule, seemingly unimportant decisions, (at the time), that transported me to whore I am.

Here at the university, at the seasoned age of 25, I worked for a man who would become the person, who would influence my next 40 years.

His name was Pete Cillo. Pete was everything I wasn't; tall, dark and handsome. He was a former Marine captain who led US Marines in Vietnam, 2 tours. He had a wonderful sense of humor, an electric personality, people wanted to be around him. I was proud to call him my friend; more about Pete later.

12:32PM

What to do? First, disbelief. This does not happen to us, ordinary people out on a Saturday. I think back to events from the US. Look for a place to hide. I didn't know where the gunfire was coming from, nor did I know from how many perpetrators; 1 or 20. Time starts to slow, eyes dart around, decisions are made. Former soldiers tell me its combat processing. I yell for Susan to follow me. We go in the back storeroom of the store. I tell Susan to duck down behind a shelf. I create a hiding spot on the top shelf of the storeroom. If someone comes in they will not look on top behind them.

At work at the U of D, my best friend, Pete left to pursue another career in North New Jersey. I called and told him I wanted to speak with him, I needed advice. So, one Sunday afternoon, he drove halfway and I drove halfway to a Howard Johnson's on the NJ Turnpike. Pete knew what was going on. I told him I was going to resign and move to Washington

State. I didn't know whether or not I had made the correct decision. Pete said, "You don't want to be 65 years old and say to yourself, I wish I had done that."

I know that I have written about what could have beens throughout. This was the first one for me. What if I do? What if I don't? I have often told kids in my later, pontificating years, when you are young you can make stupid, ill conceived decisions, you still have time to pick yourself up and start over. Pete's words echo in my ears, and my very being, since then. The Pete story gets even better. I resigned, packed my car, drove to Washington. I had been there two days when we got a call that Pete was in the hospital, and two days after that he died; Spinal Meningitis. My friend, who had the world in his hands, died at the age of 28.

Think now about fate. Think about the people who pop into your life and just as quickly pop out. Were they angels? I believe that God sends people to us to teach us one specific thing. And then leave. Think about "things that could have been." Think about if you did things different, what might be? I will always remember Pete and his words, "You don't want to be 65 and wish you had done that."

12:32PM

I run out to the clerks to tell them to lock the door, but, they don't have a key. Believe it or not, books and movies played a role next, James Bond movies and Tom Clancy novels, always be aware of your surroundings, have a plan, don't panic. A clerk tells me to run out the exit door, on the right outside the Adidas Store. The exit opens up to the rooftop car park. I run again to the back and grab Susan. She is still great, no panic, follows my direction without question or hesitation. We were blessed, we weren't ensnared, and later the remaining hostages would be kept in the Adidas store, trapped, tortured, beheaded, castrated, killed; another momentous decision.

Chapter 5

Escape…from more than one predicament

I moved to Washington DC, where I met the first Mrs. Strazzella. Fate continued to play a role in my life, 9 years of unhappiness and I escaped to Northern New Jersey.

12:35 PM

The exit door outside the Adidas store opens up to the rooftop garage, and we followed a panicked, screaming crowd from the Casino onto the roof. My first thought; we are out! Still hyper alert, I look for an escape route. We run to the corner of the garage, gunshots still being heard in the mall. A crowd of people are bunched in the corner. There is an open window frame that people are climbing up and into and jumping. I realize, no, too many people, where are they jumping we are four floors up? The garage is full of cars surrounding by a wall about 6 feet high. There is no obvious escape, or even an obvious entrance/exit ramp. In the corner near the door we came out of is a small café, with plants and a 3 feet high wall.

I move to North Jersey, to a small one bedroom apartment, no refrigerator, no furniture, but I am happy. I have a new job, a new start; I trust my fate, to fate. One Friday night in February I stop at the local bar on the way to my luxurious unfurnished apartment, and I meet the now, love of my life, Susan. She is just out of the hospital, with her friends. Apparently they feel sorry for me and they tell her to give me her number; Fate, once again. A year later I tell her if she married me she would see the world; she believed me, I didn't. A few months later we are married, and our life of adventure begins.

12:37PM

I am still looking for a way out. Susan is with me, watching, and waiting. I am processing the surroundings, looking for an exit, we are still not safe, and we still hear multiple gunshots. There are children everywhere; there was a cooking event for kids being held. The crowd is bunched and pushing in the corner. They are trying to get up and through an opening, a sort of window in the wall. I realize that Susan will not be able to get up in the window, nor jump to safety. I think, well, we'll have broken bones, but alive. I decide against it and tell Susan to run. Time continues to slow down; blood is being pumped to extremities, my vision narrows. My eyes dart from one scene to the next, trying to decide what to do.

Chapter 6

Travel, adventure, life.

Susan and I both appreciate and love adventure. Before long, we begin to travel; Easy, civilized places at first; Paris, Italy, Spain, Poland, and Europe. Eventually we branch out; drive thru Germany, and Belgium, trains to Budapest and Vienna. Our wanderlust is being fed and nurtured by the excitement of it all. Turkey, Jordan, Egypt, Greece, Estonia, Latvia, Russia, Slovenia, Bulgaria, Romania, Morocco, all become grist for our mill. We in next to no time we take overnight trains; Amsterdam, Stockholm, Hamburg, and on and on. We wander the small towns and villages of France and Italy; we visit the quiet reflective majesty of the US cemetery in Normandy. We love the people, the food, the wine, the outright excitement of travel. We see and experience the goodness the world has to offer, we also see, the evil. We cry in Auschwitz, Majdanek, and Dachau, we see the evil that existed in the world. There is still evil. I remember the day in Majdanak, cold, dreary, and wet. No one else was there, I saw the ovens, I was the only one in the room, alarming, eerie, and frightening.

Soon, we longed for more adventure. We headed to the Far East. I made naan in a restaurant in New Delhi, saw and experienced the Taj Mahal, and learned of the story of love that built it. Wandered the streets of Mumbai, where generations live on the streets in boxes. Travelled Vietnam, from north to south, Hanoi, Da Nang, Hoi An, Hue, Saigon, the Mekong Delta, followed the footsteps of US Marines across the Perfume River. We craved more, people would ask us; why there? And we would say, why not. Life is not a dress rehearsal. We were some of the first Americans in Myanmar, magical names form the past, Rangoon and Mandalay, with our picture on the road to Mandalay. We fought the heat to wander the grounds of Angkor Wat, built in 1125. We ate deep fried spiders in Phnom Penh, marveled at the grandeur of Hong Kong, wrestled with the crowds in Tokyo. Still people asked, why. I got to the point of doing videos, and showing them in the conference at the office, everyone could not believe we did it. Somewhere deep in their questions, was concern; were we pushing our luck? We never had problems, either through shear dumb luck or naiveté. We stayed in a tent in the rain forest in Malaysia, and walked the trails to the beach between the Gila monsters and the monkeys. We somehow ended up on occasions in Laos and Thailand. There was the three weeks in China, I am sure we ate fried snake or something. We travelled so far out that people wanted our pictures they had never seen Caucasians.

And the travel continued. We watched the penguins in Australia, and went snorkeling the Great Barrier Reef, and soaked in the beauty of the beaches of French Polynesia. By this time we were up to 45 countries and counting. We talked of visiting 100. Oh, I forgot South America, steaks and Malbec by the tons in Argentina, sampled the wine in Chile and Uruguay. Everywhere we were intrigued by the people, their lives, and their food. We always felt safe. I often said that people around the world wanted the same things; a better life for their children, a chance to get ahead if they worked hard.

Chapter 7

An inch

<u>12:39 PM</u>

As I process the scenes, in the corner, an abrupt explosion. A grenade explodes in the corner in the crowd, scores of people probably killed. I had a thought that I am grateful that we did not get bunched up in the corner trying to jump. Was that a grenade? I also think, I can't believe this is happening. So that's what that sounds like; really loud, smoke, and screaming, more intense than before. Suddenly I feel something, gravel, dirt hit my head. I sound whizzes along my ear, I swear a train just roared past. I instantly assume it is shrapnel from the grenade. Just then; the smell hits me, it is gunpowder. I know that smell. An inch, if I stop a split, micro second sooner?

Fear, yes fear hits me, an emotion, difficult to explain. We talk of fear, but does any ordinary person ever experience it? We speak of fear of confrontation, fear of the unknown, fear of rejection, but deep down in your DNA fear? There is that fear of everyday life, but this is different. I am so afraid for us that I am numb. For the first time I realize, we could die here. We could die, in a parking garage, in a mall in Kenya.

May 2013

It was that thirst for travel and adventure that brought us to Africa. We are running out of places to go. Susan never wanted to go to Africa on a safari, but, the "you only live once" mentality took over, and she said let's go. Months of planning went into our trip. Friends marveled at their experiences in Africa. We had numerous vaccinations; yellow fever, typhoid, Hepatitis, tetanus, polio, and pills for malaria and food poisoning. We used the last of our airline miles and flew first class. It was the trip of a lifetime, almost the last of our lifetime. We bought safari outfits, the proper hats, treated all our clothes to ward off the mosquitoes and bugs, and still we couldn't wait to go.

12:40PM

The bullet "had my name on it," but he missed. He didn't miss the young girl 3 feet to my left. I watched in horror and disbelief as she was shot, in the head. To my right, another man shot and fell like a rock. Confusion, screams are all around. I am constantly scanning the area, keeping an eye on Susan as I yell for her to run in front of the cars and duck for cover. I don't see where the shots are coming from. How do you watch someone, get shot in front of you? It is an event an ordinary person doesn't see every day. I felt no emotion, only fear? A lousy inch, he misses. Was God watching out for me? Not my time? All questions that I would try to examine later. Susan saw the spark of the bullet that missed me hit the wall behind me, and it sparked red. She told me later that she thought that it was blood and I was dead. In tears, she told me that if I was dead, she was standing up next; she was not going home without me. I cannot describe the emotion that accompanied that statement; then, and even now. There is smoke, panic, dust, screams, and confusion.

Chapter 8

HE, appears

I turn and yell to Susan to run. Before she runs, I whisper in her ear that I love her. Somehow, I wanted the last words she may hear, to be that I loved her. At that point in time, I felt we were going to die. I follow closely behind. She is running along the front of cars pulled into parking spaces. She is able to run about 5-6 cars until, a car pulled so close she can't go any further. I watch her as we are stalled in our escape; she ducks down under the front bumper. I am under the front of a car, one down from her. With me, under the car, is a young Kenyan woman with a crying infant. I think, I need to move, the baby is drawing attention to this car, my car, my hiding space. I can't move, yet. The terrorist appears in the front, very calmly, methodically, and deliberately shooting into the crowd. He is a young black man, dressed in black combat pants, a vest, festooned with grenades, and extra magazines. He carries an AK-47. Unexpected, yet rational thoughts go through my mind. I am aware that I am keenly observant; watching and mentally recording every detail. I know it is an AK, he appears very well trained, very disciplined. He is firing in semi-auto mode, conserving ammunition, picking his targets. If it was fully automatic, we would all be dead. He has a prescribed amount of time; to terrorize, and kill.

Our lives were normal, and ordinary. We bought a condo in Bayonne, New Jersey, Susan's hometown. I worked for

Stroehmann Bakeries in NYC and later promoted to the corporate office near Philadelphia. Susan commuted to various art direction jobs in Manhattan; life was great, and ordinary. Shortly after being promoted we moved and bought a house in Princeton, New Jersey. We loved our house and Princeton. Our two cats, Bud and Yoshi, become our surrogate children. We both worked hard, saved and I retired in 2011. Life was even better, we moved to Asheville NC and even more dreams came true. Susan opened her own studio, and she was even happier, living out a childhood dream. I worked part time at the YMCA, we did everything we always dreamed about. Life is grand.

12:40PM

Our terrorist stops shooting and delivers his manifesto. I am under the car, watching him. I can only see him from the chest down. He tells the Muslims to leave, and they stroll past laughing and texting as if it is a normal afternoon stroll. The terrorist calmly reloads. I remember the distinct click of a magazine being released and reloaded. He claims that; "you are in my country killing our grandmothers." The Kenyan army is indeed in Somalia as part of a multinational force hunting down the terrorist organization, Al-Shabab. A father, with his two daughters on either side of him, are trapped standing up, nowhere to go. He talks and tries to reason with the terrorist, to no avail, he shoots him, dead, in front of his children. I still am watching in disbelief, still hyper alert, watching Susan.

Chapter 9

Lying in dirt, grease, and blood

12:50PM

Not sure when it happened, but he leaves. I get up to go over to where Susan is hiding. I hide on the other side of the car. I cannot get fully underneath; but I know he is looking for white skin, white people. Susan is under the front bumper between two big Kenyan men. I try to put my arms under the car and hide my head. Except for moaning of the wounded, it is deathly quiet. Reflexively, I try to brush off the dirt on my pants; and I think what am I doing? Soon, even the moaning stops. All you hear is the rustle of the breeze and dogs barking in the distance.

12:55PM

I am a few away from the girl that got shot in the head; I watch as she bleeds to death. I think; wow, blood is really red. Fortunately, I can't see her face. Her phone keeps ringing, calls she will never answer, from relatives, from friends who have heard and are worried. She has fallen in an awkward position; I try to emulate that position in case HE comes back, hoping that he will think I am dead. I coolly and rationally decide if he comes back and walks this way, I am rushing him, I got nothing to lose, I am going to go out fighting.

1:00Pm

Waiting for the police, who never show? The Kenyan men next to Susan are calling the police, saying where are you they are killing us. Later I found out, Kenya does not have a 911 system. We still hear gunfire from within the mall. I look down the car at Susan, she is hunched over, but calm, watching me. I give her the signal to watch me.

Waiting. I think still, am I going to die. By this time, however, I somehow deep inside I felt we were going to make it. You think back thru your life, not flashbacks, but events. The fear is incredible, your heart is racing, I am hot and thirsty.

Waiting. You think of your life, material things acquired that don't matter now. Your predicament feels detached and unreal. You watch under the car for HIS boots to reappear, praying for them not to do so.

1:15PM

Waiting. People ask if I prayed; I can honestly say no. Despite the mess we were in; I guess I felt, somehow, we were going to live. I am watching Susan, worried about her, still not knowing what to do. I watch a man get up and run from under a car towards to exit ramp. I remember the extraordinary look of abject fear on his face. Did he make it?

1:30PM

Waiting. I have an intense feeling of helplessness. I wish I had a gun. I am not trained, but I know how to shot. It has been quiet for 15-20 minutes. The shooting has mostly stopped in the mall, and still no sirens, no police, no help. The dead girl's hair, long and beautiful, is blowing in the breeze, her blood is still wet and intensely red in the sun shine, and her phone is still ringing. I am thinking, what if I have to pee, and what an ordinary thing to think about now. It is still so quiet, except for the occasional gun shots in the mall. We found out later, those shots were people being executed. The terrorists were asking the hostages a question; who was Mohammad's mother, wrong answer meant instant death.

1:40 PM

Waiting. I whisper to Susan at the end of the car, to follow me, we are going to move. I feel we are trapped. I am exposed; she is not close to me. The two Kenyan men next to her hiss to "get down." They are afraid to draw attention to "our" car. We both get up and run to the next car. It is a Toyota SUV, one car down from our previous spot. I absurdly think to myself, it's difficult to determine the make and model from underneath. However, it is a big car with enough room underneath for both of us. I laugh to myself, here is Susan crawling around under a car, something I never would have imagined I would ever see. She is a trooper, no hesitation, followed me immediately. I worry that I am making the correct decisions, one wrong move, and dead. It is leaking gas on us from bullet holes; we are covered in dirt, blood, and now gasoline. It is quiet, we touch, alive, but afraid.

Chapter 10

Escape!

Thirty eight years zoom by. It's true that life is short. I have an ordinary life, grow up, work, retire. I am extremely fortunate. I worked for the same company for 32 of those years, and I have a pension. At 60 years of age I retire. We are deliriously happy. Susan has her studio; I have a part time job and wonderful, fun, new friends. There is more time to travel. We escape the cold, the cost, and the taxes of the Northeast. Asheville becomes our home and we take to Asheville like an old friend. It is vibrant, young, hip city; Restaurants and music, the mountains and fresh air, preposterously friendly, loving people. Church is important, Sunday; businesses do not open until 1pm, after church. We move to an apartment in a where we walk everywhere, restaurants, movies, the Y. I thank God every night for our life and health. And now, lying under an old Toyota, gas, blood, and dirt all over us, I wonder if that is it for us. Stop and think for yourself. You have just seen the face of evil, and lived. Is this just a short reprieve? Are you next? The anxiety is incredible.

1:45PM

Waiting. Still under the car; watching and waiting. I am watching for "his" feet to return; still no help, no police, no sirens, nothing. At least we are together, under the same car, I am thinking that at least we will die together. I am sad and at peace at the same time. Sad because life is over, and not how I expected, at peace, we are together.

Suddenly, I see a white male walking towards us. I know instantly it is a good guy! He is carrying a Glock handgun, with obvious expertise and self assurance. He quickly bends down and checks a person who has been shot, and inexplicitly takes their picture. We discover later he is an ex-SAS and former Irish soldier and his partner, a former Irish Ranger; they both work for an oil company in Nairobi. When they arrived they found bodies strewn across the balcony of a ground floor café, and gunshots. Shots could be heard from the rooftop car park. They climbed the external fire escape that led to the Java coffee shop, and our rooftop refuge. They yelled for us to run and escape. Many people were too terrified to move, a source of guilt for me in the ensuing weeks, as I felt I should have gone to people and dragged them to move. I yell to Susan, go, and follow me. I get out from under the car and run to the other side to pull her out. I glance at the wall where the father was shot with his daughters. One is maybe catatonic or dead but in any case, not moving, I yell to her to run, she does not move. I guess she is dead. I run. Susan is running behind me. I want her behind me until I understand what is going on. Although our run across the parking lot was only about 50 feet, it seemed longer and took forever. I kept thinking that it looked like we were going to escape. I was hopeful and wary, half expecting the terrorist to reappear, watching the good guy yell for people to run to the Java coffee shop.

Some people refused to move, what's wrong with those people; this guy is getting us out! In a few weeks, I would feel guilty about not helping to get them to move, about not helping our good guy to get them out.

1:50PM

About 15-20 of us are running across the lot towards the coffee shop in the corner. On the outside of the shop, they have made a small outdoor seating area. It is an outdoor area carved out of the corner of the roof parking lot. Around the seating area is a wall, approximately 3 feet high, made of cinder block. Along the top, they have placed potted plants. I wonder where we are headed as we follow behind. I reach the wall and scrabble over and I turn to help Susan over. As I turn, I see my un-athletic wife leap over the wall like a gazelle running the hurdles. I almost stop to laugh. Once inside, I see 20-30 people hiding behind the counter, on the floor, some crying, some hysterical, all frightened. In the hallway behind the counter people are bunched up, no one knows what to do. I turn to Susan and tell her to run back out, it is too crowded and we would be trapped.

The good guy reappears, and tells us to run to the back of the shop and down the fire stairs. He turns and yells, "Is anyone armed?" A big black man next to me says, "I am," and I watch him hand over my head to him a silver plated model 1911 semi-auto .45. I will never forget that shining handgun being passed to the good guy. I will also never forget his next words; "I'll hold them off, you get people out."

I have reached the age of 63. I am an avid reader of history, and especially military history. I have read countless stories of heroism; World War II, Vietnam, Navy Seals. I have often thought to myself, how I would have been in those dangerous, and life altering and threatening situations. Would I have been a coward or brave? **"How can I be a hero?"** *Better yet, "how can I prepare and equip myself to be a hero in those moments in life that demand it?"*

I have seen the quote somewhere, "we are all brave, but a hero is just brave 5 minutes longer." What kind of person runs into danger instead of away, what makes a fireman run into a fire and not away, what makes our military risk everything for us. Churchill once said," "We sleep safely at night because rough men stand ready to visit violence on those who would harm us."

"I'll hold them off," will forever be etched in my memory of this day. Afterwards, we prayed that he lived; we saw his picture in the paper days later, helping people out of the mall, he was alive; A Hero.

1:55PM

We run to the back of the coffee shop. In the corner is a door that exits to the back fire stairwell. We start down the stairs. There is crying, hysterics. Two men are carrying a young girl with a bullet wound to her foot, she is bleeding profusely.

Unbelievably, there is a teenage girl, running while talking on her cell phone. Everyone is yelling to her shut up and run!

Our little band of 20 survivors race four flights down. I reach behind me to grab Susan, we hold hands tightly. Finally we reach the bottom of the stairs only to stop at a closed door. No one there to direct us, no one knows what to do. I run to the front and crouch down on the floor. I gingerly, carefully open the door. It is clear, we all rush out. We are in the bottom floor of the enclosed parking garage, and no obvious exit to the outside. There are mall guards milling around, no sense of the danger that rages above. There is a white man concealed by a parking barrier holding a 9mm handgun; watching and waiting. The guards tell us there is no way out here; I quickly look around. Plenty of cars, plenty of places to hide if need be.

I turn to our group and tell them to go back up one flight. Inexplicitly, the two guys pile the wounded girl in the elevator. They'll be trapped! Too late to stop them, we all race back up one flight. Susan is hanging in, I see worry on her face, but also determination, she follows me again unquestionably and without hesitation.

The next floor up, the door is closed. I crouch down again and peer out. There is an open garage door and sunshine! A policeman with an automatic weapon is gesturing us to run this way. I reach around for Susan we both run for the door. The Kenyan man shouts for us to stay low and hug the outside wall, they are shooting at us from the roof. Out the door we see the remnants of the earlier siege, food, plates and a big box of salad dressing; its contents litter the ground near the outdoor café kitchen exit.

We are out! Relief, exhilaration, exhaustion. We made it out alive! Outside; no cops, no army, no ambulances, nothing.

Chapter 11

A guardian angel

As a child in St. Thomas' Grade school we had catechism class every day, from grade 1 to 8. We answered our daily questions by rote; "who made you? God made me." And like all children raised by nuns we believed in guardian angels. Everyone had one, we truly believed our guardian angel sat on out right shoulder and kept us out of danger. Did you ever think that in your life you meet a person, however briefly, and that person, an angel, was put there to teach you one thing, explain one lesson? It has happened to me, Pete Cillo, of the admonition to live life, was the first for me. In Kenya, I met another.

We wandered out of the mall looking for help. Crowds of Kenyans were watching and waiting. People were streaming out of the mall in groups; wounded, crying, hysterical, and horrified. At the end of the street, we hugged; I did not want to let her go. Still not believing what happened, still not believing we lived.

We are dirty, thirsty, and bloody. We walk down the street in a daze. I try to call the hotel driver, my phone does not work. A Kenyan woman sees us, an angel in disguise. She asks if she can help. She sits us down in the shade, calls the driver and keeps him on her phone until he arrives. As we follow her to the car, I am wary. Wariness will be always with me now. She leads us to the car, kisses us both, and says she will pray for us, and says God bless you. We called her our Kenyan Angel.

Back at the hotel, the entire staff is waiting for us in the lobby; they know where we have been, many are in tears. Our driver is upset, even angry. He says this will hurt Kenya; it will hurt the people who depend on tourism for a living. He is kind and caring, a decent hard working man, who is troubled. In the hotel we head to the bar, we are surrounded by the wait staff, and head of hotel security, they are all concerned and supportive. Our waitress from the previous night, a sweet, young Kenya girl, holds Susan's hand with an unexpected, touching, tenderness.

I feel the need to call people in the US and tell them we are OK, we are alive. Most still don't know what has happened. The event is on TV in the lounge, we are incredulous, and we still have a difficult time believing we were there. Like the US, the event will consume the TV 24/7 for the next week.

As we sit, and try to calm ourselves, the hotel security tries to assure us that we are safe here; but are we really? We are dirty and bloody. We go back to our room, and the hotel housekeeping staff comes for our clothes and shoes. Over the next day, they are returned to us, spotless, always with a smile and prayer, and they won't accept a tip.

Over the next few hours, we try to decide what to do about our safari. The tour company comes to visit to offer words of support. They assure us that we will be safe. Late that night, we hear noises; Susan jumps at every noise, every sound, sounds like a gunshot. At midnight, we decide to go home. I think the day's event has finally hit us, the reality that we were that close; an inch, a minute, a second, a step, a turn…. *to death.*

Chapter 12

Returning Home

The next evening we are going home, we need to be home. We both feel numb and apprehensive. The Nairobi airport is a mess, chaos. Three months before there was a fire at the international terminal, the arrivals and departures were in a temporary building. In fact the British Air departure gates were a tent on the tarmac. We meet an American woman, trying to get out. Her husband is on a different flight, and she was in Nairobi to identify the body of her pregnant friend. Her friend was one of the first people killed at the mall outdoor café; both mom and baby were shot and killed. There is intense sadness, we don't know what to say, we all want the hell out of Kenya.

Finally, on the plane, we are tense and touchy. We feel a sort of heaviness, difficult to articulate, but omnipresent. People next to us, boarded earlier and they have used all the overhead bins around our seats. They are smug and self important and I am in no mood for obnoxious assholes. There are words. I am ready to snap, a kind of pretense to our next few weeks at home.

We change planes in London at Heathrow airport, and we are relieved to be back in civilization. As we de-plane to make our connections, we are greeted by 4-5 Anti-terrorist agents of

Scotland Yard. They are there to help gather data for an international effort to identify the Mall attackers. At this point, no one agency is sure that the attackers haven't escaped by mingling with the people still finding their way out of the mall, two days later. In addition, there is speculation that the mall attackers were led by a woman, the so called, "Black Widow." Her husband was killed in a suicide attack in London that past summer. The Scotland Yard detectives asked us to tell the story, again, in detail. They take our pictures, and DNA, and tell us the FBI may be in touch. The event to us becomes even more surreal.

Finally, we arrive home in the United States. In the Charlotte airport, we are relived and tired, and grateful to be here, and alive. Within 48 hours of the event we are home. The "Vacation of a lifetime," doesn't seem so important, "we are safe."

Chapter 13

The Aftermath

(CNSNews.com) – President Barack Obama has described al Qaeda as having been "decimated," "on the path to defeat" or some other variation at least 32 times since the attack on the U.S. consulate in Benghazi, Libya, according to White House transcripts.

One day after the Benghazi attack that occurred on the 11th anniversary of 9/11, Obama spoke at a campaign event in Las Vegas on Sept. 12.

"A day after 9/11, we are reminded that a new tower rises above the New York skyline, but al Qaeda is on the path to defeat and bin Laden is dead," Obama said in Las Vegas.

I mentioned in the prologue that this story "would not be a commentary on Politics or terrorism." However, I cannot help but comment. Most Americans, 99.99% will never be involved in an event that we experienced, therefore, to those people, al Qaeda on the run *is* their reality. It is not ours. We come home frightened, we are frightened of Muslims we see with headscarves, frightened of crowds, frightened of malls. To us, there is no such thing as a moderate Muslim. Perhaps that feeling is wrong, and perhaps it will change, but for now, that is how we feel.

We are not prepared for the reception upon our return. At the Y the next day, I am shocked and overwhelmed with the outpouring of love. Not only from the people who know us, but everyone. Hugs and tears, that's all we know for a few days, they all know our story; they all said they prayed for us. People tell us that we were the subject of prayers and sermons in numerous churches all over Asheville. I think; this is America, this is the America where I was raised.

Everyone also wants to hear the "Story," we can tell it, in great detail, it doesn't seem real to me. Everyone is visibly touched and moved, and for that we are grateful.

On Tuesday morning after we have been home for a day, I awake to the headline on the Asheville Citizens Times; "Locals survive Kenya Mall Attack." Susan and I become even more famous. Local TV stations send video crews and reporters to the Y and to Susan's studio. Radio stations call us every day. Unbelievable to me, one TV station gets through to the Executive Director of the Y and has the impudence to ask her, "If we were the kind of people who would make that story up," Mainstream media at its best, but I tell them all we are not looking for our 15 minutes of fame and we want to be left alone.

Many of our friends encourage us to see a doctor, they are worried about PTSD, and I am not. Friends tell me that we basically experienced combat, and I can understand why they say that. We eventually do, and the doctor was encouraged by our answers and demeanor. The fact that we got home so quickly after probably saved us.

We see more and more people every day, most cry when they see us, and we end up comforting them. Some say they are sorry, and they are happy to see us safe and home. Some are asses with such inane comments, "I hear you had quite a time in Kenya, betcha won't go back there, ha ha." Sorry and happy to see us, seems to be the best.

Yes, sorry, we love you and happy you are home and safe.

Chapter 14

What did we learn, the practical.

What did we learn? In my mind, what we learned is probably the most essential ingredient in the book. I would describe our learning in several pieces, some practical, some esoteric.

Here we go; what we learned about people, what we learned that is practical and useful, what we learned about ourselves, why were we saved?

First, let's review the practical, and quite frankly, the easiest to talk about.

Always be aware of your surroundings. Maybe I read too much, maybe I was a secret agent in a past life, but, I always reconnoitered my surroundings. In a restaurant, theater, stadium; where are the exits, where are the pinch points where the crowd will rush to go. What if the is a fire, or some other event, like ours, that creates a need to escape, where do you go?

- Be aware of conspicuous or unusual behavior in airports, bus terminals, etc... Do not accept packages from strangers. Do not leave luggage unattended. Learn where emergency exists are located. Think ahead about how to evacuate a building, subway or congested public area in a hurry. Learn where staircases are located. Notice your immediate surroundings. Be aware of heavy or breakable objects that could move, fall or break in an explosion.

These are the precautions that are recommended by experts. I can assure you from personal experience, self assurance in the absence of professionals, make decisions without second guessing, stay away from the crowds.

YOU, must be responsible for your safety, you cannot save the world. You are not a trained professional, and you cannot, cannot, save everyone. Guilt will be part of the aftermath.

What we learned about people.

Upon our return, we met and spoke to so many people who knew us or knew about us. However, we were shocked, and quite frankly, dismayed at the number of people who are oblivious to the world around them. Our politicians cater to the lowest common denominator, and I can understand why. So, many people, do not read, do not read newspapers, do not watch or listen to the news, and they get their opinions and information from someone else. On numerous occasions, we encountered people who never hear about any worldwide event. We are both shocked and dismayed by this lack of awareness.

Chapter 15

The esoteric; fate, God, why are we here?

Just about every discussion upon our return involved some talk of fate, destiny, and angels. My belief is there is no such thing as fate. That is my belief. To me, fate implies some sort of life path that is predetermined. Many people said that it was, "not our Time." I also do not believe that. Maybe there is fate and destiny, maybe there is a specific timeline of our lives, and maybe someday we will know, maybe not. I do believe that we were saved that day, perhaps by angels. I do believe that God saved us. Every discussion also involved the talk about why, why were we saved.

As you have read throughout the story, I believe that at some point in my life, someone popped in for a brief moment, and left a very specific impact on it. I firmly believe that we were saved for a reason; I believe we have a responsibility to share our experience, and here's why.

People have asked; did you pray. I can remember distinctly I did not. I also remember distinctly the thoughts that went through my mind, crouching under a car in that mall. I felt, yes I felt, very strongly that we were going to LIVE. I cannot explain that feeling. I also remember thinking I was not going to make bargains with God; you know, please save me and I promise I will be good and go to church every day, etc. I somehow knew that wasn't necessary. If you live your life the way you are supposed to live, bargains at the last minute are not necessary. I have told that story many times since, maybe that's what I am supposed to do. Many people I met wanted to offer their own assessment of why we were saved; some even wanted me to speak with their psychic, weird.

So, here's what I learned; angels, I think, watch over us, God, perhaps, has a plan for us and we possibly were saved for a reason, life is fragile, it can be taken away at any unplanned, unexpected moment, the best and sometimes the worst come out of people when subjected to absolute fear, and make no mistake; there is good and evil in this world.

Chapter 16

The guilts, or the "should I haves?"

So, we are home. Time helps heal. For the first couple of days I did not want to let Susan out of sight. There was some comfort in being together. We continue to tell the story, over and over, and it gets easier to tell. I start to have the "guilts." I lie awake wondering; should I have helped the guy who saved us by dragging the catatonic people out? Should I have gone back up the stairs and helped get people out? Should I have checked people who were shot? The images and thoughts are straight out of the movies, I realize I am not trained or responsible, at times I feel like a coward. It is a deep, unrelenting guilty feeling. I picture myself as the brave hero, unafraid, yet in fact, I worried that I was perceived as the opposite. I ask Susan if did OK, she says we are alive aren't we? That statement somehow does not seem to be satisfying.

Every man wants to be tested, save the day, and come out strong. It is in our nature, our very manhood genes. I finally realize that I am the only one questioning what I did; nevertheless, the thoughts still occasionally haunt me. An ex-SEAL I met tells me I did good, makes me feel a little better, but….

Chapter 17

"What could have been?"

Minutes and inches

Weeks pass, we are much better. However, I am more often racked by all the "what could have beens." I spoke in the beginning about second chances, what you would do over.

We were supposed to be spending the day in Addis Ababa and catching a late flight to Nairobi. Instead, they found us a flight leaving right away. Instead…. we arrived in Nairobi early Friday morning, not late Friday night. We had a full day to do nothing, so we went to the mall, if we had just kept the original flight, we wouldn't have had time to go the mall.

We wanted to just hang around at the hotel, but someone suggested we go to the mall.

We planned to leave for the mall at noon; instead, we were early and left at 11:45. If we had left at noon, we would have arrived when they stormed the entrance; **we would be dead**.

We got to the mall and entered; in the lobby was a coffee cafe, and we talked about having a coffee and decided against it, if we had stayed; we **would be dead**.

We went to visit the basement grocery store; when the lights flickered we decided to come back later. No one in the store seemed concerned; the cash registers were still working. I just thought, oh well, its Nairobi. Two of the three Al-Shabab came thru the back loading dock. Everyone inside was killed or tortured, some eviscerated, some castrated. Had we stayed, **we would be dead**.

Susan and I strolled the upper floors. We stopped to shop in a small boutique. The clerk was bored, I was bored, and Susan tried on several tops. We were there 20-25 minutes. Had we stayed five minutes longer we would not have made it to the top floor, I don't know how we would have gotten out; **we would be dead.**

On our connection flight through Addis Ababa, Susan finally gave up on the shoes she brought with her. She went to a store in the airport, not really a store, but some merchants sitting on the floor. For $45 dollars she bought what looked like Adidas shoes. When we reached the third floor of the mall we said, I wondered if the shoes were real and what did they cost? In that store, we heard the original gunshots. Eventually this was the store where the terrorists held the last of the hostages, 4 days later. Had we stayed and hid, we would have been caught, tortured, **and we would be dead**.

As we hid in the back storeroom of the Adidas store, I braved a look outside. It was then I saw everyone running towards the exit. Had I stayed 3 minutes longer, and not looked out, we would have been caught, tortured, **and we would be dead.**

Once outside, I saw the crowd massed in the corner trying to climb through an opening in the wall. For a split second I considered doing that also. But, it was crowded, where were they jumping to we were on the top floor, and I consciously thought; Susan cannot climb that wall. That corner was the first to be hit with a grenade. Had we ran to the corner with the crowd, **we would be dead**.

As we ran along the wall, crouching low, I turned towards the explosion. Thinking shrapnel, it was in reality a bullet. Had I stopped 4 inches sooner, the bullet that missed would not have, and **I would be dead**.

The decision to run in front of the cars along the wall was unintentional, it just happened. Had we decided to run in front to try to run away, that is where the initial people were shot. Had we followed, **we would be dead**.

In a life, so far, of 63 years, how many times did these kinds of scenarios happen? Dozens, hundreds, perhaps thousands of time our lives were changed, perchance for the better, perhaps not, most we may never know. However, for us, these events will always, as long as we live, be remembered because we knew that those inches, and minutes were the difference between life and death.

Chapter 18

We go one, we lived.

And so, months later, our lives are back to normal. We went to Italy for 2 months in November, unafraid and happy. Yet still.....in the back of our minds is that 90 minutes in Nairobi. We are more wary of crowds; going to the mall was actually a bit disconcerting. And we still travel. Travel brings power, wonderment and love back into your life

"We live in a wonderful world that is full of beauty, charm and adventure. There is no end to the adventures we can have if only we seek them with our eyes open."
— Nehru

And so... finally, take this from an ordinary guy, in an ordinary life, caught in an extraordinary event. I can only offer to you the most important thing I learned...please, take this, remember it, and use it, for I will always remember when

Susan said; "I thought you were dead, I was standing up next, I wasn't going home without you."

Hug the people you love, everyday; tell them you love them, everyday, you never can know what awaits them as they go out the door.

I